THE WEIGHT OF A FEATHER

Stephanie Ní Thiarnaigh is an Irish multidisciplinary artist and poet based in Drogheda, Co. Louth, Ireland. She co-hosts the Irish Mythology Podcast and is a co-founder and member of Boann Art Collective. Her work explores folklore, mythology, memory, power, class, labour, the state, and the otherworld. Her work has been published in *Splonk, Queerlings, Red Ogre Review, Pile Press,* and elsewhere. This is her debut poetry collection.

ISBN: 978-1-916938-39-7

Cover designed by Stuart McPherson

Edited by Charley Barnes

Typeset by Aaron Kent

Broken Sleep Books Ltd
PO BOX 102
Llandysul
SA44 9BG

CONTENTS

The Weight of a Feather

Stephanie Ní Thiarnaigh

Broken Sleep Books

Keep in mind, I am not a historian.

So I will recount facts as best as I can, given limited resources and understanding.

— Layli Long Soldier, 38

I unite your limbs, I hold your discharges together, I surround your flesh, I drive away the fluids of your decay, I sweep away your bᵉw, I wipe away your tears, I heal all your limbs, each being united with the other; I surround you with the work of the weaving goddess, I complete you and form you as Re.

— Spell 145, *Egyptian Book of the Dead*

If we know, then we must fight for your life as though it were our own—which it is—and render impassable with our bodies the corridor to the gas chamber. For, if they take you in the morning, they will be coming for us that night.

Therefore: peace.

— James Baldwin, ***An Open Letter to My Sister, Miss Angela Davis***

INCIDENT 1: THE PRIEST AND THE TEENAGER
The Deaths of Father Hugh Mullan and Frank Quinn
(After 38 by Layli Long Soldier)

Here, the weight of a feather will be respected.

There is an old mathematician's riddle that poses the question: which weighs more, is it a pound of gold or a pound of feathers?

One could be forgiven for expecting the answer, like an eye for an eye, to be that of course they weigh the same. However, nothing is quite as simple as that.

An ornithologist will weigh a bird's feather as a proportion of total body weight on average being 0.0082 grams, but no two feathers are the same.

So a hen's feather might weigh 74 grams using the *avoirdupois* system of measurement, where there are sixteen ounces to the pound - a pound of course, being adjudged according to Imperial measurements invented by the English.

Previously it was the manner and custom of ancient Ireland, for grain or indeed for a hen's eggshell (weighing 55ml) to be the relative standard of measurement - but I digress.

Gold, precious metals and gems, you see, weigh less under a troy system, in which there are 12 ounces to the pound.

All things being equal to mass, a pound of feathers is 454 grams and a pound of gold is 373 grams. Therefore, the answer to the riddle is that the feathers are technically heavier. The weight of a hen's tooth is certainly a different story, but regardless of body parts, it is true to say *is trom cearc i bhfad*.

If you carry a feather from Ballymurphy to Battersea, it will weigh more than when you left, and I suppose that if you carry a beret from Battersea to Ballymurphy, the inverse is also true.

To speak of Ballymurphy of course, is to get into the business of weighing hearts (and minds) as well as feathers, because it was in Ballymurphy in 1971, over the course of 72 hours between the 9th and 11th of August, the 1st Battalion Parachute Regiment of the British Army killed (murdered) at least nine (entirely innocent) civilians (without justification) as part of Operation Demetrius.

I say "at least nine" because this is the official figure. However, it could be ten depending on the system of measurement that is used, given that there was a tenth victim shot outside a Catholic Church and witnesses testified they saw British soldiers shoot towards the area, but it was not confirmed during an inquest into it in 2021.

Then again, it could be eleven depending on your system, but the eleventh wasn't actually shot by soldiers.

They didn't waste a bullet on this one because the British soldiers simply inserted a gun into Mr. Paddy McCarthy's 44 year-old mouth to stage a mock execution, after which he suffered a heart attack and died.

It may interest you to learn at this juncture that the traditional unit of measurement of a bullet is in grains, however modern rubber bullets, being made of rubber, are weighed in grams.

Operation Demetrius was a British security forces operation during which suspected members of the Provisional IRA were rounded up and interned, that is to say, imprisoned without trial.

For our friend the mathematician, rounding will mean replacing a number with an approximate value that has a shorter, simpler or more explicit representation. It is often done to obtain a value that is easier to report and communicate than the original, but it can also be done to avoid being (misleadingly) precise in measurement.

Almost 2,000 people were interned in this period, but it is more accurate to say that it was actually 1,981, with 342 of these being arrested on the 9th August 1972.

A further 7,000 people were displaced from their homes.

The Parachute Regiment of the British Army carried out Operation Demetrius in a chaotic manner, informed by poor intelligence.

Many (most) of those arrested were not members of the IRA.

In Belfast on the 9th August, a British Army press officer, Mike Jackson, who would later become the head of the Army, said in his autobiography, *Soldier: The Autobiography*, that those killed in the shooting were republican gunmen.

In 2021, the judge found in the inquest we are discussing here, heard over 100 court sitting days, that this was not true.

The six civilians who were killed (murdered) by the British Army on the 9th August 1971 are as follows:

Francis Quinn (19), shot while going to the aid of a wounded man.

Father Hugh Mullan (38), a Catholic priest, shot while going to the aid of a wounded man, reportedly while waving a white cloth to indicate his intentions.

Joan Connolly (44), shot by three soldiers as she stood opposite the army base, and she might have survived had she been given medical attention sooner, but she lay injured in a field for several hours.

Daniel Teggart (44) was shot fourteen times.

Most of the bullets entered his back as he lay injured on the ground.

Noel Phillips (20), shot as he stood opposite the army base.

Joseph Murphy (41), shot as he stood opposite the army base.

Murphy was subsequently taken into army custody and after his release, as he was dying in hospital, he claimed that he had been beaten and shot again while in custody.

When his body was exhumed in October 2015, a second bullet was discovered in his body, which activists said corroborated his claim.

I have not counted the exact number of times I have seen this but I recall another Catholic priest was shot in Springhill in Belfast by the British Army alongside four others. He had also been waving a white flag as he tended the injured victims which included a thirteen year old girl.

There is a famous photograph of a priest, Bloody Sunday in Derry January 1972, waving a blood-stained white handkerchief as he escorted a group carrying a mortally wounded protestor, after British troops opened fire on demonstrators.

Hankies are weighed in ounces and the unit of measurement for the weight of blood is litres and millilitres.

The exact measurement of the weight of a Priest's blood saturated peace-handkerchief is a question for the mathematician.

Witness M152 applied to give testimony on the condition of anonymity, citing risk to his life were his role in the British Army and Prison Service to become public knowledge. He submitted medical evidence of his high blood pressure in order to support this.

Blood pressure is measured in millimetres of mercury (mm Hg).

On 10th August 1972, Edward Doherty (28) was shot by British soldiers while walking along Whiterock Road.

This is not a full picture.

It was not simply a lovely summer's day otherwise uneventful except for the shooting.

The RUC duty officers' reports for the 9th and 10th of August 1971 paints a picture of the scale of unrest and strife as follows:

Across Belfast alone on 9th and 10th August 1971 it is recorded that there were approximately 12 explosions, 59 shooting incidents, 17 reported deaths, 25 reported injuries, 13 incidents of rioting, 18 reports of arson and other reports of civil disorder of various kinds.

Many residents in Springfield left their homes as crowds had gathered to attack them.

One man who escorted his wife from their home when approximately one hundred people had gathered at their back garden, returned the next day to find two bullet holes in his bedroom and bathroom window, and a bullet from a Thompson sub-machine gun was removed from an internal wall with a pen-knife.

On 11th August three civilians were shot;

John Laverty (20) and Joseph Corr (43) were shot at separate points at the top of the Whiterock Road.

Laverty was shot twice, once in the back and once in the back of the leg. Corr was shot several times and died of his injuries on 27th August.

The tenth unfortunate soul was John McKerr (49), shot in the head by an unknown sniper while standing outside a Catholic church and died of his injuries on 20th August.

As outlined, eyewitnesses said that soldiers were seen shooting but the inquest failed to establish who killed him.

The coroner noted that a more specific finding was not possible, largely due to "*an abject failing by the authorities to properly inquire at the time.*"

I have already referred to Mr. McCarthy and his mock execution.

A number of difficulties arose during the inquest relating to the British Army's poor record keeping practices that impacted the correct identification of who shot the deceased.

Radio logs were missing as well as records of ciphers of soldier identities relating who said what in statements from 1971.

Indeed, the British Army's own regulations dealing with maintenance and issuance of weapons and armory from that year could not be located.

This is especially unfortunate given the British Army's rich history of record keeping with archives dating as far back as 1760 being available in Kew Gardens.

I should however say that as of June 2019 the Coroners Service had identified around 800 soldiers potentially able to assist the inquest.

The inquest located contact details for 567 of these soldiers (168 were confirmed as dead), and this list was eventually whittled down to 60 individuals, described as a core or target group of military witnesses.

Two months later, the British Ministry of Defence provided the Coroners Service with a further source of potential witness details in the form of a late stage disclosure of un-paginated, ill-defined Data Preservation Repository Records that included the names, service numbers and regiments of no less than 4,773 British soldiers who served in the north of Ireland in the 1970s.

Helpful - although no information particular to Ballymurphy was provided.

One hundred and twenty seven individuals gave inquest statements.

Two witnesses failed to cooperate with the Inquest despite the issuing of subpoenas for their attendance, with the rules of the Coroner court not providing a legal basis to compel their attendance in the jurisdiction of the Coroners Service of Northern Ireland.

Coroners in the north of Ireland are of course appointed by the Lord Chancellor, formally the Lord High Chancellor of Great Britain, who is the highest-ranking traditional minister among the Great Officers of State in Scotland and England in the United Kingdom, nominally outranking the prime minister.

The Lord Chancellor is appointed by the sovereign on advice of the British Prime Minister.

Lady Chief Justice The Right Honourable Dame Siobhan Keegan, acting as coroner, set out to fulfil legislative obligations looking at the how, when and where of these deaths.

The why of the question was not specifically referred to. However, a reader may extract their own conclusions in this regard upon noting the how of it all - in that the question arose in asking the how of whether it could be established if the deceased *had acted in a manner that would arouse suspicion from the multiple regiments in operation in Belfast at that time.*

Let us begin with the death of Father Hugh Mullan.

Mr. Bobby Clarke, who survived being shot, has at various points outlined how in the course of the fighting in the area he had been moving women and children to safety and said that British soldiers watched him carry a child to safety and when he put the child down, they shot him in the back.

It was Father Mullan who attended to Mr. Bobby Clarke when he had been shot.

In any event, Father Mullan was shot and died there and then, so Mr. Clarke waited in the grass in the dark until he was taken from the field just under two hours later.

Father Hugh Mullen was born on the 9th April 1933, sharing a birthday with Gian Maria Volunté who you may know played the villain against Clint Eastwood in *A Fistful of Dollars*.

Both men were less than one month old when Dáil Éireann passed the Bill to abolish the Oath of Allegiance, no longer promising to be loyal to the British monarch, and his or her heirs and successors.

Father Hugh Mullan was from Springfield Park, adjacent to the waste ground in which he died.

Father Mullan was from a close-knit family and had enjoyed sailing on Strangford Lough in his living days.

Coincidentally, ex-serviceman M154 who requested to not attend the inquest due to potential adverse health effects that it would have on him (no medical evidence offered initially) and that of his wife (no medical evidence offered), maintained strong connections with the north of Ireland due to a sailing pastime.

Lieutenant General Sir Harry Tuzo, then General Officer Commanding Northern Ireland, wrote to the Bishop to express his regret at Father Mullan's death bringing the *"very warmest sympathy of the Army in Northern Ireland in the loss which the church has sustained. If you could find a way of conveying these feelings to Father Mullan's relatives, I would be most grateful. I need hardly tell you of the sorrow which yesterday's events as a whole causes me. I hope to do something today, possibly with the help of some of your priests, to guard against a recurrence tonight."*

Less than one year later in July 1972, Lieutenant General Sir Harry Tuzo ordered around 30,000 British troops in to what were considered "no go" areas for the army (22,000 British Army, and 5,300 Ulster Defence Regiment) in Operation Motorman in which a child, Daniel Hegarty (15) was shot at close range twice in the head in Creggan, Derry by a man named as Soldier B.

Soldier B was charged with murder but the charges were dropped in 2021, after judges suppressed key evidence on which the prosecution was to rely.

An unarmed member of the Provisional IRA, Seamus Bradley (19), was also shot by a British soldier during Operation Motorman as he ran across open ground and it was found that he would have survived had he been administered first aid or transported to a hospital.

However, the deaths of Daniel Hegarty and Seamus Bradley are not being discussed here and I must attempt to stick to one dead teenager or priest at a time.

Frankie Quinn, despite his young age of 19, was already married with one baby, and had been unable to get to work on the morning he died due to the rioting.

Father Mullan when he died was noted by the pathologist to have been wearing his black clerical clothes and a white cotton vest, very heavily bloodstained, and a pair of blue underpants, also heavily bloodstained.

Father Mullan was of average build and 5'8" and was recorded as having gunshot wounds in his chest, one of which was fairly neat and circular and 6mm in diameter, with a 1-2 mm reddish abrasion under his left nipple, and an oval wound 14mm x 8mm on his right side.

He was noted as having a further wound on his lower forearm (14mm x 12mm) and an elliptical gaping wound (58mm x 28mm) on the inner side of the forearm.

In summary, he had two gunshot wounds on the left forearm, one on each side of his chest, a furrowed wound on his right arm, and gunshot wounds both on his abdomen and left buttock.

A round is a military term for a unit of ammunition, made up of a cartridge case, primer, powder, and bullet. It is also called a "round", or "load".

Sometimes this is incorrectly called a "bullet".

The doctor concluded it was probable that the wounds were caused by only two bullets fired from a height by high velocity weapon(s), likely to have come from the same general direction (and possibly from the same weapon) and likely to be rapidly (but not immediately) fatal.

The cause of Father Mullan's death was recorded as (a) lacerations of the right lung, liver, stomach and intestines due to (b) gunshot (high velocity weapon) wounds to the chest and abdomen.

Father Mullan, having received two or potentially three gunshot wounds, would have remained alive and able to vocalise for at least a few minutes.

Having been shot and removed from the waste ground to Royal Victoria Hospital, Royal Ulster Constabulary Officer Alan McCrum took swabs from Father Mullan's hands and his clothes.

These were sent for a forensic examination which concluded that there was no lead residue on him.

Ballistics experts who later reviewed the evidence said that it was not possible to determine definitively the exact number of bullets which may have been from rifles but potentially a pistol calibre bullet. It was noted that Father Mullan's clothing had not been examined for close range effects.

It could not be determined from wound reviews alone where exactly the bullets that killed Father Mullan had originated from but it is clear that Father Mullan was (is) the same amount of dead regardless of whether it was two bullets in his body as three or even four.

The word bullet actually has the same origins as the Latin word "*bulla*" meaning "round thing", which eventually became boulette in French (cannonball, small ball). This Latin word also gives us "bull" meaning the highest document issued by the pope (a sealed document). I am minded to tell you this, as Father Mullan was a teacher of the Latin language and highly regarded in teaching in general.

Francis Quinn, who died alongside Father Mullan, was born 19th April 1952, the day on which the sun begins its sojourn into Taurus.

1952 was the year that Peig Sayers travelled to Dublin for the first time in her life and the first year Samuel Beckett had staged *Waiting for Godot*.

During the original autopsy Francis Quinn was wearing a brown cotton sweater with long sleeves that was buttoned up to the neck and had blood stains around the collar and in a patchy fashion elsewhere. He also wore a pair of calf length brown laced boots, brown socks, blue jeans and a leather belt. He was wearing white underpants.

Francis received a gunshot wound to the back of the head that made the shape of a 14mm x 8mm oval that was just between the top of his neck and hairline.

Generally speaking, pathologists or medics use a ruler to measure the wound. However, I have read more recently that there is some sort of computer software that can be used now too.

Francis, dad of one baby, also had bruising on his cheeks and the copper jacketed 7.62 calibre bullet, which was 29mm long and 9mm in diameter, was retrieved from overlying the outer surface of his upper jaw.

Jacketed is a firearm term to describe a bullet that is made of softer lead surrounded by another metal, usually copper, that allows the bullet to penetrate a target – a skull for instance – more easily.

Three experts reviewed the evidence and considered in some parts whether or not the bullet had in fact travelled through another individual before reaching the back of Frankie's (yes, he was known as Frankie) head as it had slowed down in passage prior to hitting him.

This bullet may have made its way to Frankie's skull via Father Mullan, however they were not the only two shot on that day so it might have made its way to its eventual landing point via another route.

What is clear is that both men died around 9:00pm that evening, and there had been much conflict between the residents of Springfield Park and Springmartin Road.

A large peace wall divides the two areas these days.

Many of the Springfield Park residents fled from their homes due to the disturbances which may have involved hundreds of people, and it was said that there were maybe a small number of IRA men about the place during the day, however these gunmen were not in the waste ground or in the vicinity of Father Mullan.

The shots fired by the British soldiers into the waste ground were not in response to shots fired at them and there was no risk or perception of risk that the priest and the teenager were a threat to the British soldiers.

In fact what actually happened was that as people fled their homes amid the chaos and shooting, Father Mullan went to assist the injured in the waste ground.

A man, Mr. Clarke (who survived), had been carrying a child across the field and he had been shot.

The child's details are unknown but the average weight of a seven year old is around 23kg.

It is not unreasonable to assume a child weighing the average weight might feel heavier when avoiding bullets.

Arís, is trom cearc i bhfad.

Father Mullan went to anoint the man, and while or shortly after giving him the commendation of the dying, the priest was shot.

Francis Quinn who had gone alongside the priest to assist the injured was also shot, and the bullet that lodged in the back of his skull travelled perhaps at first through Mr. Clarke or Father Mullan.

In any event, Father Mullan had two bullets in him when he died and Francis Quinn had one and the inquest found that this bullet had travelled through another person first.

The British Ministry of Defence suggested that this death was possibly as a result of UVF sniper fire but the Lady Chief Justice was satisfied this was not the case, and that both men had been shot by the British army.

The British soldiers had suggested that Mr. Quinn had been in the field with a gun wearing a white shirt.

The judge (correctly) found that this was not accurate.

The RUC had suggested that Mr. Quinn had been shot in Moyard flats and his body subsequently moved by an unknown person. The judge reasonably asked if Mr. Quinn was the person in the flats who soldiers had cause to shoot at, why indeed had they shot him in the back of the head?

Francis Quinn did not stash a gun and have a quick costume change before his autopsy.

It was still light outside and everyone shooting had a clear view that the priest and the teenager were not armed and were merely helping the injured.

There was so much firing from 3 Queen's Rifle Brigade and the 2 Para B Company that there is a credible theory that at one point they were in fact shooting at each other, and the injuries sustained by the deceased were caught in the crossfire.

The truth is that the investigation was hampered by the fact that many military participants did not give evidence through deciding not to attend the inquest or applying to be excused.

Some soldiers gave evidence akin to a see no evil/speak no evil style, stating that they had seen nothing because they were on balconies that were on *the ground level.*

Peculiar indeed.

The memoir *Soldier: The Autobiography* by General Sir Mike Jackson weighs 798 grams, or 811 grams depending on the edition, which is almost the same as 100,000 feathers, or potentially the weight of two human hearts depending on their health and stage of life they are in.

The inquest found that Fr. Mullan and Francis Quinn had done nothing to provoke their own deaths.

The average heart weighs between 200 to 425 grams and is a little larger than the size of a fist.

The weight of a feather will be respected.

POGROM

We are clenched fists marching
down a mountain straight through
Bombay Street, where lace nets
billow like tall ship sails in glassless
windows, snatch squads ready to riot,
we roll out our CS carpet. We are
here to restore order. Our chieftain
signals to fall in. Voiceless grunts — we obey.
Choppers glide beyond the reach
of stone projectiles, as a band plays
The Sash in the distance. A mercenary
can just about catch a bouquet
of engulfed gridlock through a charcoal
veil. Support the scorched earth
strategy of patriots. We do not wait
and see. This is war.

IT IS A POEM, NOT A TESTIMONY

I say that I am not a story, or
authority on the history
that creeps inside your tv screen,
mediated by the well-paid.

I say that I am not an alchemist
and this is not a verse,
designed to proselytise
your thoughts into dust.

I say that I am not a testimony
of what really happened. I
am just a poet who wrote
what comes after.

FÁG AN BEALACH (POEM OF MOTTOS OF BRITISH ARMY REGIMENTS)

We assist by watching, to hit the mark

Swifter and more keen than eagles,

Exemplo ducemus (By example shall we lead)

In futurum videre (To see into the future)

Venture, adventure, ready, aye ready, utrinque paratus (Ready for
            anything)

We Sustain, fear naught

Quis Separabit (Who Shall Separate Us?)

Per mare, per terram (By sea, by land)

Per diem, per noctem (By day, by night)

Ubique! Quo fas et gloria ducunt (Everywhere! Where right and
            glory lead)

Celer et Audax (Swift and bold)

Cede nullis (Yield to none)

Per Ardua Ad Astra (Through Adversity to the Stars)

Nec aspera terrent (Difficulties be damned)

Pristinae virtutis memores (Mindful of former valor)

First in, last out, everywhere

                        unbounded

Throughout the night,
            we strike

Death or glory

Nemo me impune lacessit (No one provokes me with impunity)

Death

    or glory

        We strike.

adverb

1. during the period of time preceding a particular event or time: *Joan had eight children before she was shot three times by British soldiers while trying to help a fatally wounded teenager | Joan welcomed the soldiers to Belfast before things turned nasty.*

2. *archaic* in front of someone or something: *While the shooting continued in Ballymurphy soldiers were indiscriminately arresting people and putting them in vans, with other soldiers running before and behind.*

conjunction

1. in advance of the time when: *Joan remained alive for a period after being shot by three or perhaps four bullets in the leg and face saying 'I can't see, I can't see' before she died of her injuries | It was 2:00am before soldiers moved her body.*

2. in preference to (doing a particular thing): *Many of the British soldier witnesses would die before they would cooperate with the inquest proceedings.*

preposition

1.   during the period of time preceding (a particular event or time): *Despite the shooting outside, Joan had to find her children before going inside | the day before yesterday | before the war.*

2.   in front of: *The saracen appeared before them, with its passengers armed and ready | Did her life flash before her eyes?*

3.   in front of and required to answer to (a court of law, tribunal, or other authority): *The coroner could not compel the soldiers who shot at innocent civilians to appear before the inquest | The British Government intends for no criminal prosecutions of soldiers relating to Ballymurphy to be brought before the courts.*

4.   in preference to; rather than: *A State that will protect its soldiers before all else.*

RIFLE

we have begun a game of forty forty, unaware,
dirty thirty standing, unmoved but armed. tea ladies
threaten. dawn chorus clanging. tap tap on a rifle

as we stifle laughs. this is for you and you. cheeky chappy
trigger-happy. forty forty i see joan connolly behind the tree
each pop will stop mammy in her tracks. forty forty save me

because we aren't going back. sing song where's your
mother gone. dispatcher body-snatcher. all night long in
the scratcher. ping pong bing bong i'm not wrong. tag, you're it.

FIRST WORD

Listen—

A baby babbles in the living room to her Mamó

Later under siege,

she says *Dada* for the first time, and everyone smiles.

WOULD YOU MIND PUTTING YOUR GUN DOWN FOR JUST A WEE SECOND?

I have no clue what some appropriate
methods of polite request are.
I am thinking about the time I
heard a wain crying in the field.
Crawl to the ice-cream van.
Think of the taste of a 99.
I usually have brain freeze.
Do you think you can make it
through the hole in the fence?
I wanted to be an artist when I
was little, and draw a cone
so accurate, you would
try and lift it from
the page in front of you.
I shout at the them to stop
but they keep going,
continuous fire
to counter an unseen threat.
I plead for an hour. *Can you please stop?*
There is a child out there.
A military act of generosity.
You have two minutes—Go!
Collect the baby with a bullet
and his brother in a 120 second
ceasefire while the cold takes root
in my soul.

SMOKE BREAK

What should you think about a man who writes
a deadman's skull
was used as an ashtray
when his comrade
says, this fantasy
merely sells books?

How should we think
about what it means
to have the idea of
putting your cigarette out
on the inside of
someone's head?

What would you think

if your best friend said

this happened?

The intention of it

is real, even if the act of it is not

The impossibility of knowing
which is true
is worse.

I HAVE NOT EXTINGUISHED A FIRE

when it should burn
says the negative confession. You
are a long way from Duat in Ballymurphy
Squaddie, brother, singer, son,
a boy determined to leave a home,
to make a life for himself—always
the first to open the door for old ladies,
help the child who is hungry, neat dress
ready to take orders, freshly trained in
deciding on a coin toss the fate
 of a man who unexpectedly
reminds you of your Uncle
John from the back, an inion
hook a bulls-eye, you set your sight
on this Legionnaire gate-keeper, one
of your own, and he lurches forward
falls on the fence and you, a jackal
satisfied for one minute turn
to your pack leader to lick
your lips, and he says *Good Boy*
and scratches behind your ear
while the sun splits the stones
at your feet.

preposition

1. throughout the course or duration of (a period of time): *Over 300,000 British Soldiers served in the occupation of the north during the years between 1969 and 2007* | *The peak of deployment was reached in the 1970s, during which 21,000 soldiers were stationed there*

2. at a particular point in the course of: *An unarmed civilian, Noel Phillips, was shot at least three times by at least two British soldiers, with two shots behind the ears, execution style, during Operation Demetrius in Ballymurphy*

ORIGIN

late Middle English: present participle of the obsolete verb *dure* 'last, endure, extend', via Old French from Latin *durare* 'to last' (see duration).

MORRÍGAN WAITS ON WHITEROCK ROAD

She observes chaos
rigid above a tree trunk barricade,
a low hum of fear surrounds exposed ghosts,
and to a Sapper says,
No, it is not the time
to raise your sterling sword

Ignoring her, unease grows,
stones fly with
wings—she sees him
lean out of the carriage, ready to strike
against an imagined phantom. She approaches
a house, watching a boy watch a soldier
watch his carefully aimed magazine empty
in the body of a wrong man in the wrong place
in the wrong time
like acorns falling too quickly
from a diseased oak

Revolted by the scene she screams
as Tech Duinn welcomes another. The Sapper
will remember this but will solemnly,
sincerely, and truly declare it differently
fifty years from now, before his God,
avoiding a truthful recounting
of bloodthirst—the moment
of execution, remembrance of
seeing a man realise

he is about to die as claret bubbles

foam in his lips

Exuberant with power in the box, he does

not notice the Morrígan

waiting for him

BALLYMURPHY BUZZFEED QUIZ

1. You are a teenager living in Ballymurphy at home with your brother and father. Your mother is in Butlins with the other children. At 3.00am you hear shooting and people are shouting outside that there are British soldiers coming down the road. Do you

   a) try and go back to sleep using the pillow to drown out the noise of shooting *[Proceed to Ending 1]* or

   b) get up to speak to your father *[Proceed to Question 2]*

2. It is now 4.00am and amid the sound of plastic bullets being fired outside, you hear what sounds like moaning coming from your garden. Do you

   a) Go to the front door of your house to see what is happening *[Proceed to Question 3]* or

   b) Stay inside your house *[Proceed to Question 4]*

3. You are now at your front door and you realise the moaning is coming from an injured man on the other side of your garden hedge. He says he cannot move. He tells you to not open the gate or try and help him as you will be shot. You do not have a phone that you can use to call for medical help. The gunfire outside escalates. Do you

   a) Consider risking being shot while entering your garden amid the gunfire to assist the man *[Proceed to Question 4]* or

   b) Retreat to the relative safety of your house *[Proceed to Ending 1]*

4. British soldiers enter your home and arrest you and your teenage brother. As you are being removed, you see the injured man that the moaning sound had come from has now either crawled to your garden or possibly been dragged there by the hair by British soldiers. He has been shot in the back and is covered in blood. Do you

    a) Continue to protest your arrest to the British soldiers interning you without trial *[Proceed to Ending 1]* or

    b) Cooperate fully with the British soldiers who have referred to you as an 'Irish Bastard' while beating you and your brother in your garden and thank them for their service in protecting your community *[Proceed to Ending 1]*

Ending 1

You and your brother are both interned without trial. You will be beaten so severely by members of the army that you will need to take 6 months off work and eventually you will receive compensation for your injuries. You will be required to relive this repeatedly for various inquiries and interviews, but in fifty years' time the British Prime Minister Boris Johnson will apologise for the manner in which *investigations* were carried out into the shooting of the man from your garden. The man from your garden will be found to have been innocent of any wrongdoing and the soldier who murdered him will never be identified. Thank you for playing!

SUMMER HOLIDAYS

We return home from blood-soaked lanes,
retreat to busted bannisters and demolished wedding china.
Smashed shards of window glass make
a delicate tiara on a doll. Our neighbour said
Hold your empty palms up and they will know
We mean no harm, and so we do.
We watch grown men beat children in gardens,
trampling across mangled clematis. They take doors
off hinges for sport. Not long before, I spoke to one
of these uniformed protectors when I
was out digging the flowerbeds and
I offered him—someone's child, some tea.
Have you ever smelled jasmine bloom in
August? You wouldn't leave anyone thirsty.
Basalt columns of soldier's shit strewn across
saturated beds and the scent of piss belts
me in the face like an ammonia tide. Acrid
waves roll across the carpet. Rise
and fall with each slow breath. In the bedroom,
unseen by beach hunters, I start to clean.

BELFAST HAIKU

A dark quiet street

Saracen drives to the door

Bang! All dark again.

IN THE MATTER OF A DEATH THAT OCCURRED IN AUGUST 1971 AT BALLYMURPHY, WEST BELFAST

Inquest into a Death at Ballymurphy, 9th August 1971 – Present Schedule for Hearing Week Commencing 26th November

Monday 26th November

Preliminary Evidence: Death of Truth

No.	Name	Evidence	Called or Read Under Rule 17 of the 1963 Rules or Spell 125
1	Edward Heath, Prime Minister	Political	125
2	Reginald Maudling, Home Secretary	Political	125
3	William Whitelaw, Secretary of State for Northern Ireland	Political	125
4	Brian Faulkner, Prime Minister of Northern Ireland	Political	125
5	Mike Jackson, British Army Press Officer	Military	125
6	Derek Wilford, Commander of 1st Battalion Parachute Regiment	Military	125

7	General Ford, Commander of Land Forces in Northern Ireland	Military	125
8	Lieutenant-General Harry Tuzo	Military	125
9	Usekh-nemmt, Assessor of Maat	Maat (Falsehoods)	125
10	Am-khaibit, Assessor of Maat	Maat (Those who are slain)	125
11	Neba, Assessor of Maat	Maat (Utterances)	125
12	Hraf-haf, Assessor of Maat	Maat (Those who cause tears)	125
13	Unem-snef, Assessor of Maat	Maat (Deceit)	125
14	Her-uru, Assessor of Maat	Maat (Terror)	125
15	An-hetep-f, Assessor of Maat	Maat (Men of Violence)	125
16*			
17*			
18*			
19*			

---

* Readers may enter their preferred witnesses in spaces 16-19, including the author of this book, to provide evidence, bearing in mind that they may themselves one day be required to provide evidence relating to an inquest or judgment, or present for the weighing of a heart against the feather of truth in the coming forth of days.

Thursday 29th November

Reading into evidence:

Application for anonymity and screening (Soldiers X/ XX/ XIV)

Statements on behalf of Maat

FIRST CIGARETTE

Light—
A young man spreads a pinch of tobacco in a flimsy paper and rolls

Later under siege,
he is relieved to find it where he left it on the windowsill.

As part of the British Army's efforts to control the population of Belfast following the Ballymurphy Massacre and Bloody Sunday, and the ensuing widespread community resistance to the occupation and oppression of the Catholic and nationalist communities, a plan was developed in 1972 named *Operation Playground.*

Recognising the absence of facilities for children in working class areas of Belfast and noting that Catholic children had restricted access to normal playing fields, parks and facilities, and recognising the 'expense' in building these facilities, the *Operation Playground* memo was written by the British Army outlining a joint military, RUC and civil development project in part answer to the situation.

The British Army proposed that, for babies under three, a project would be developed establishing mostly unpaid babysitting groups, with one group per high rise flat.

For those aged three to five, playgroups would be organised by local people and supervised by the NSPCC and Belfast Welfare.

For those aged five to eight, two projects were suggested, the first being play centres and the second being play sites which would be simple 'bomb' site play areas, erected by government, military and police where the children would '*entertain themselves.*'

For children aged eight to fifteen it was suggested that they should access the same spaces as above at different times but additionally, a range of other activities along more '*manly lines*' would be arranged in military and RUC establishments to '*train these age groups for their future lives.*'

The memo outlined that Limited Access Streets should be defined, where delivery vans and occupants' vehicles would be allowed on streets, but no other vehicles. It also set out that the location of babysitting groups, play groups, play centres, play sites and limited access streets would be held by Tactical HQ.

Maps were provided to illustrate. It set out that retired servicemen would be the keyholders of play areas, responsible for cleaning the sites and also tasked to '*act as vigilantes.*'

The memo also had a communication strategy noting the importance of engaging with family men and women, mothers over 30, and children – concentrating especially on the under 8s.

STRAY BULLET

Bullets roam the streets in packs observing. One breaks away
from its tribe to search a

      a bin and our pockets. It meanders carefree

         down the road and an MP names it 'Protection'

for a community under lupine siege, sturdy in
extreme unrest. Outside a church gate, in the absence of place and

company to enclose a feral heart, this wild beast
lets loose. A bullet wants to belong

      Bullet, strayed from the farm, seeks a home

      Bullet just wants to be loved.

Who will place a poster in a shop window asking *Have you
seen this bullet? Reward offered.*

      Watch how they deny owning that which

         foams viciously at the mouth.

COMMUNITY HALL OF TWO TRUTHS

In the Hall of Two Truths
there are forty-two gods ready
to witness their names be recounted and
a jumping sacred scarab who might hold down
the type of heart
whether wicked or righteous,
that would betray the words
of its keeper,
who will confess
what he has not done in living.
But if the heart weighs more
than the feather?
Be truthful
or
be
devoured.

LOVE IN THE TIME OF LORD CARRINGTON

On Wednesday 22nd September 1971, one month after the Ballymurphy Massacre, Lord Carrington, British Secretary of State for Defence, outlined his pride in the way the British Army have responded to 'a most unpleasant situation' and asked 'What do they really think their position would be if the British Army were not there in Northern Ireland? Can they honestly say that they would be safer in their homes if no British soldier was in Northern Ireland?'

A 1977 letter from Labour Home Secretary Merlyn Rees to then Prime Minister Jim Callaghan later revealed that Lord Carrington had ordered the torture of 14 men, who had been taken at gunpoint from their homes in 1971 and held without trial. The 14 have long been known as "The Hooded Men" and have campaigned since their release in the early 1970s for an official acknowledgement that they were tortured. The methods they were subjected to included the Five Techniques: prolonged wall-standing, hooding, subjection to noise, deprivation of sleep, and deprivation of food and drink. In 1976, the European Commission of Human Rights ruled that the five techniques amounted to torture. In 1978 the court ruled that the techniques were "inhuman and degrading" and breached Article 3 of the European Convention on Human Rights but did not amount to torture. This ruling was cited by the United States to justify its own interrogation methods, which included the Five Techniques. British agents also taught the five techniques to the forces of Brazil's military dictatorship.

In 2021, the Supreme Court of the United Kingdom found that the use of the Five Techniques amounts to torture.

Unruly subjects will line up in chaotic streets
named for the empire. Time to put manners and

discipline on those who do not know how good
they have it. Is anyone surprised at how a savage

responds to kindness? Appalled at how women
hurl foul-mouthed insults? How many babes

fire missiles from arms, toddler-sized stones
skimming deftly across the barricades? An army

stands ready to act for as long as it may take
to teach a lesson to the wilful. Let them decide

how long that should be. Nobody would not be
compelled to raise a hand to civilise disorder if

they would simply do as they are told. We see, this Irish
problem, thorn in Commonwealth, clearly–shame upon

the decent, moderate and law-abiding. They do not
understand our love. We shoot, and sweep the bodies of their

dead: sniper, mother, recalcitrant. A village of eavesdropping
curtain twitchers refuses to mind its own business.

Watch the island, how these lawless children ache
for the cane; quarrelsome, obstinate; in their incessant rebellion

not realising, we only do this because we care.

FIRST KISS

See—

Two Ballymurphy teenagers unaware of joy's delicate edges

Later under siege,

memory of a kiss stuns like flares in the sky

WHEN YOU DID NOT WANT TO SEE BUT YOU CANNOT UNSEE IT

what can you do, but recall. A bell cannot unring a song that
          cannot be unsung
by petrol xylophones and baritone bricks who harmonise with a
          gravel choir
and a clave that executes four loud cracks: Accidentals? There is a
          reason there is
no such thing as a 4/3 time signature. It does not sound right to

our ears, in the same way the liquid crescendo will not seem right
          to the eyes.
A conductor can control his first violinist with a baton, or his eye
will announce the first beat in a bar, to a rapt audience waiting
          beside
our bored concertmaster who plays the same starting note for the
          thousandth time.

It is frustrating to have a tune stuck in your head, when you do not
know its name. Let us train our ears so we might know the melody
performed by thirteen wilting flowers and candles before the
          creaking double
whole note of a garden gate. Let us conduct ourselves accordingly.

AN FINNÉ

A chroí mo mháthair
Ó, mo chroí féin,
Ná éirigh suas i m'aghaidh mar fhinné,
Ná cuir i mo choinne sa bhinse,
Ná sceith rúin, os comhair an Ard-Bhreitheamh deiridh

A FOUND POEM IN THE YELLOW CARD (1971)

RESTRICTED

█████████████████████████████████████

███████████████

█ These █████████████████████████████████

█████████████████████████████████████

████████████████ soldiers ████████ open fire ████████

████████████████ on the spot.

██████████████

█ Never ████████████████████████████████

██████████████████████████

████████████ try to handle the situation ████████████

████████████████████████████

████████████████████

███████████████████████████████████

████████████████

███████████████████████████████

█████████████████████████████████████

█████████████████████████████████████

████████████████████████ Commanders ████

████ may ███████████████████████████

████ order █████████████████████ a round in the breech

████████████████████████████

█ Automatic fire ████ used against ████████ targets ████

███████████████████████████████

████████████████ is ████████████████████████

████████████ employed as effectively. ████████

█████████████████████████████████████

███████████████████████

you

must:

not

think

there is

a

way to protect yourself

from

fire without warning

in your area,

At

road blocks

Ask him why he is there,

the circumstances

do not justify

fire

██

████████████████

██

██

██

███

at the first opportunity.

██████████████████████████

███

██████

AFTER | ˈɑːftə |

preposition

1. in the time following (an event or another period of time): *Our Nuala was never right after the massacre | After a while she would not speak about it | It would be hard to find peace after witnessing that*

    • in phrases indicating something happening continuously or repeatedly: *Day after day they kept shooting us*

    • *North American* past (used in specifying a time): *The front door was kicked in and the room filled with cs gas about ten minutes after five.*

2. behind: *A neighbour went out to help the injured and dead, shutting the door after her, but they shot her too.*

    • (with reference to looking or speaking) in the direction of someone who is moving further away: *She shouted after the Brits bringing elderly men away in vans*

    • in phrases referring to making somewhere clean or tidy again after the actions of a person or animal: *The women had to clean up after soldiers who had shit in the children's beds | They would prefer to just tidy up after kids playing*

3. in pursuit or quest of: *They're chasing after justice this past fifty years*

4. next to and following in order or importance: *In the State's order of priorities truth comes after denial.*

5. in allusion to (someone or something with the same or a related name): *John Laverty was named after an uncle who had fought in World War I.*

   • in imitation of: *A Guantanamo interrogation technique after the Five Techniques of torture sanctioned by the British Government*

conjunction

during the period of time following an event: *Operation Demetrius ended in disaster after the British Army's indiscriminate shooting, arrests and subsequent torture galvanised the community's resistance*

adverb

at a later or future time; afterwards: *He asked for a ceasefire to evacuate the children soon after the Paras started firing | In the minutes after Paras placed an unloaded gun in Paddy McCarthy's mouth and pretended to shoot him, he had a heart attack and died*

adjective [attributive]

1. *archaic* later: *The British Army and British government did all they could to cover it up after years.*

2. *Nautical* nearer the stern of a ship: *The after cabin of HMS Maidstone.*

PHRASES

be after doing something

Irish be on the point of doing something or have just done it:
The Army are after shooting at the women up at the school

after you

a polite formula used to suggest that someone goes in front
of or takes a turn before oneself.

after all

in spite of any indications or expectations to the contrary:
*Despite what the British Army had told the public, each person
they killed in Ballymurphy was innocent after all, and this was
confirmed in a later inquest*

FIRST BLACK FOREST GATEAU

Taste—
A usually fussy grandad takes a slice to be polite

Later under siege,
he thinks of the tart cherry syrup dancing softly on his tongue in
delight.

BLITZ

Defenders of empire

Defenders of realm

Realm of possibility

Realm of monarchy

Monarchy of fear

Monarchy of plantations

Plantation of stories

Plantation of Ulster

Ulster says no

Ulster says never

Never surrender

Never again

Again, can you repeat that?

Again, we've been here before

Before internment

Before the war,

War of attrition

War of independence

Independence of mind

Independence of state

State of me

State of you

You in the back

You in the black

Black Mountain

Black op

Op Sec

Op Tempo

Tempo of a city

Tempo of a heartbeat

Heartbeat of a lover

Heartbeat of a newborn

Newborn blade of fresh grass a child holds between his small

thumbs and uses to make a whistle

Newborn dawn at the break of a day

Day of reckoning

Day of mourning

Mourning of a lost opportunity

Mourning of a lost love

Love in a time of liberation

Love in a time of crisis

Crisis of the soul

Crisis of poverty

Poverty of imagination

Poverty of empathy

Empathy of others

Empathy of someone who might actually listen for a change

Change is inevitable but also the foundation of new beginnings

Change is a natural response to trauma

Trauma

Beginnings

MAAT'S HEARING OF THE 42 CONFESSIONS ACCORDING TO THE PAPYRUS OF BALLYMURPHY UPON THE DEATH OF A BRITISH SOLDIER

Now that you have died elderly in your quiet sleep, look your own god in the eye and tell him, Soldier, what sins did you commit in Ballymurphy?

Was it you who mugged a passerby and rifle-butted him in the face?

Tell us what you took during your time marching on Springfield Road. Do not hold back.

Admit to the men and women and children you have slain. Tell us your cipher, Soldier.

Was it you who stole food from their shops? Or kicked the fish barrow into the road?

Was it you who purloined offerings and desecrated graves in a cemetery?

Or was it you who stole the property of the gods? Whose home did the twinkly trinket on your mother's mantelpiece originally come from?

Let us read the Judgment of Inquests alongside the Judgment of Maat, and ask, what lies did you tell and for whom? Did it serve you? Make you whole? And are you at peace?

Again, I ask, were you the soldier who prevented deliveries of food?

Was it you who called them *Irish Whores* and *Fenian Bastards*?

Or was it you who laid hands on women who did not want it?

Did you make them weep? Did you care?

How many hearts have you eaten?

How many men have you attacked? How many times did you squeeze the testicles of terrified teenagers while they were spreadeagled against the wall of the garden in which they took their first steps?

It is a simple question: are you a man of deceit?

Do you think of having burned a family home as having stolen land?

Did you eavesdrop on family dinners from underneath kitchen windows?

Have you slandered an entire people?

Have you been angry without cause? And for what? Are you at peace?

Was it you who debauched wives? Or shot them as they went to buy cigarettes?

Denigrated little girls for fun? Was it you who swung a child by her ponytail like she was a Christmas cracker yo-yo?

Was it you who polluted yourself by inserting objects *inside* of others against their will?

Recount to us, who have you terrorised? Do you recall? Was it you who defecated on a baby's bed? Did you remember doing that when your own youngest moved from cot to a Big Boy Bed and you were so proud?

Tell the gods the laws of your own Pharaohs you have transgressed.

Have you been angry at a people for just *being*?

Tell us about the moment when you shut your ears to the words of truth. Repeat it. Repeat it. Repeat it. Speak louder, we cannot hear you.

Recount the curses you shouted at innocents.

Admit if you are a man of violence. Was it you who put a man up against his own bedroom window while you shot from behind him at your target?

Admit if you have been a stirrer of strife. Confess your psyops.

Tell us you acted with undue haste, how you would shoot to kill.

Was it you who pried into others' matters for your own ends, and threatened to out queer joy so a man in love might become your agent?

Tell us how you multiplied your false words in speaking before a Coroner.

Attempt to make us believe you have wronged none, and have done no evil. Was it not you who tried to put bullets in the empty pockets of a dead man?

Tell us what witchcraft have you worked against their leaders?

Tell us how you stopped the flow of water to a neighbour and attempted to pollute a river

and how you raised your voice, screaming wildly in the face of the already dying,

and how, still to this day, you curse their gods?

Admit your arrogance

and your theft of bread from the starving

and how you stole cakes intended for a wake of their dead

and without shame snatched the milk of children and treated the spirit of an entire city with contempt.

Did you slay what they believed was sacred?

Tell me, Soldier, did you slay what you believed was sacred?

Tell us these things, and we will see where we stand.

BALLYMURPHY POETRY PROMPTS

Write about Ballymurphy
Write about how it would be funny to refer to your therapy sessions
as The Boundary Commission

Consider the dinnseanchas of Ballymurphy
Write about how a place is more than its people who were murdered

Use the phrase '*When pain lays bare such cruelty*'
Use the sentence '*They fashion lies to uphold social order*'

Write about Guantanamo, drawing a line from the British Army
perfection of the art
of waterboarding republican prisoners interned in 1971 to the
present day

Write about what it is like to search for your child under gunfire
Talk about the last rites

Write about the history of waving pieces of white cloth to get
soldiers to stop shooting
Begin a poem with the line '*Halt. I am ready to shoot*'

Write about Lord Carrington approving methods of torture
Write his obituary using the stories *The Guardian* left out

Write about the soldier who lied and said there were bullets in
empty pockets
Write about tripping over a dead body

Write a poem in the form of an essay about what it is to tell a story
that is not yours
Make a found poem from the text of the Yellow Card

Write about the first child's birthday party held in Ballymurphy
after August 1971
Use the terms civil disorder, panic disorder and post-traumatic
stress disorder in a poem

Write in the voice of a British Soldier
Write about the Brit who made an 18-year-old boy get on his
knees and bark like a dog at his girlfriend in the street

Write in the voice of a child's PTSD
Write in the voice of your own PTSD

Tell the reader the number of times you cry
Realise your tears are not important

Ask what it means to persevere
Write about truth

Write about your truth
Write about the truth of others

Ask what is the meaning of justice
Write a poem attempting to measure grief

Write about the power of hope
Consider what it is to be part of a community

Write about what motivated General Frank Kitson
Write about the psychology of breaking people

Ask how do you rebuild
Chronicle how they have rebuilt

Write about the Ballymurphy Massacre
Write about the weight of a feather.

ACKNOWLEDGEMENTS

In writing this collection, I relied heavily on the documents of the Judiciary NI Inquest into Deaths at Ballymurphy 9th – 11th August 1971 as well as Ciarán de Baróid's seminal work 'Ballymurphy and the Irish War,' which I highly recommend.

There are a number of people who require special thanks for supporting me in invaluable ways in writing this book, whether it was reading drafts or making cups of tea or coming along to workshops and readings. I appreciate you all so, so much.

To Mark Hoskins, for believing the act of writing is truly sacred, and for all the love and support. Mo cheol thú. To Abhainn Connolly, for calling me a poet when I wanted nothing to do with the word. To Sarah Malone for love and friendship. To Lauren Foley for feedback, friendship and consistently encouraging me in my writing. Cathal Malone, go raibh maith agat as do scileanna gramadaí, is mór agam do chuidiú. To Ciarán Hodgers for reading early drafts of this work and responding with such enthusiasm. To Brenda McComiskey for putting me on a stage. To Cathie Shiels and Alisande Healy Orme for reading early drafts. To Paulie Doyle for never being afraid to remind me what real problems are. To Anis Dabchy, for everything. Baci! Simone Amiras Vistarini, fratello mio, grazie per la tua amicizia e per aver letto le prime bozze. Ti voglio bene! To Ciarán Quinn who read an early draft of this and responded with incredibly kind words.

To Rachel Long, whose poetry workshop I attended with the Irish Writers Centre. Rachel challenged us to write a poem 'using the facts' in the style of *38*, by Layli Long Soldier as a prompt and asked us to open the piece by stating that which would be respected. This writing exercise eventually became *Incident 1: The Priest and the Teenager*, the first poem written in this collection. I found that I could not say all of what I wanted in one poem and the rest became this book. To Aaron Kent at Broken Sleep Books for giving this book a home, and Charlotte Barnes for her exceptional editorial skills and patience in dealing with all of my crimes against punctuation.

To John Teggart who gave words of encouragement regarding the role of the arts in seeking justice. To the people of Ballymurphy and the families, friends and loved ones of those who died at the hands of the British state, thank you for persevering against the relentless and deliberate obstacles placed in your way and for teaching us all what truth telling looks like. Your grace, courage and dignity is a credit to your lost loved ones. I hope I have done them justice in this short book.

To you, the reader, for turning these pages, thank you. Go raibh maith agaibh.

LAY OUT YOUR UNREST

www.ingramcontent.com/pod-product-compliance
Lightning Source LLC
Chambersburg PA
CBHW030854090426
42737CB00009B/1231